APPLES OF GRACE: 31 Days of Inspiration for the Educator

by Cortland Jones

JAYMEDIA PUBLISHING

Copyright © 2018 by Cortland Jones.

All rights reserved. No part of this book may be used or reproduced in any manner whatsoever without the express written permission of the publisher except for the use of brief quotations in a book review.

Printed in the United States of America
First printing, 2018
JayMedia Publishing
Laurel, MD 20708

Cover Art by Cristy Sanchez-Urrutia
Cover Design by Ashlee Sasscer of Designs with Sass

Foreword

I was inspired to be an educator when I saw the learning gap between my younger brother and me. I used that as a catalyst to create a role-playing environment that would allow me to bring my brother up to par. To him we were simply playing a game; however, to me I was using my passion, limited knowledge, and compassion, to reach my very first student. That simple and impactful instance of assessing a need, implementing role play and witnessing how I influenced the learning of my younger brother reminded me that if I could teach with only seven years of knowledge, passion, and compassion there's no stopping me now! To this day, I still see that glimmer of hope and spark of thought, that I affectionately describe as a "thought bubble with fireworks" in the eyes and body language of my students - as I did with my younger brother almost 40 years ago. Now, that's what I call passion! My purpose was ignited within me, and it still burns today.

Shortly after that, I developed a need to be alone and recharge myself frequently after interactions with my brother as well as other people. That didn't seem normal to me. Then, it started to manifest in school. Luckily, I had a teacher whose passion for teaching allowed her compassion to recognize my little "personality quirk," (now known as shyness and introversion). At that time, it was crucial for my future success, that I was afforded the necessary tools and support to help me not only understand myself but also to give me confidence in knowing that it was okay, that I was not alone. Therefore, it didn't put a damper on the knowledge that I attained as a child; instead, it only enhanced what was more to come. Then, along came Cortland, and GraceToTeach! As I was home on leave after teaching and moving back to the US from Japan, I began to feel my introversion creeping back as it became harder to get motivated and get out and about. So, I found a group on Facebook for teachers in Maryland. I would scroll up and down the page, and every day I would see something that was positive, enlightening and full of compassion...just what I needed. This name, Cortland Jones, kept surfacing. I decided to extend an invitation, by messaging him, to join another group on Facebook. I needed him to help spread that spark of joy in my group for Educators of Color. Little did I know, I would log on to my page, and right there was my daily confirmation on my page. I'd read his posts or quotes, then respond with a loaded comment, as my expression, to the world, for that day! I felt that comfortable, again...but GOD!

Being an introvert causes teacher burnout more frequently with me than with my extroverted colleagues, in my opinion. Therefore, it is essential that I remain diligent in practicing the skills that I learned so early on, beginning with my third-grade teacher, to help me in my teaching career. I learned to unselfishly take the time that I need to prepare myself for my students on a daily basis as well as care for myself during moments when I need to refuel. I accomplish this with prayer and worship, meditation, music, and reading devotionals such as Apples of Grace: 31 Days of Inspiration for Teachers, along with essential oils and lots of faith. It doesn't hurt to have like-minded and passionate educator friends, such as, Cortland Jones, always there to lend a positive word, backed by scripture, and a listening ear, when needed. Just as God knew me before I was in the womb, He knew that Cortland and I would cross paths at a time in which my heart and mind needed renewed strength and compassion. During many days that I suffered from burnout he would, unknowingly, share the perfect blog post that day, to help me make it through. BUT GOD!

My thought about the three essential qualities of an educator - passion, knowledge and compassion - is that you cannot have one without the others, as they are all necessities in the journey of an educator. First, it would be important to stress the word "essential." When something is essential it is absolutely necessary to sustain- such as food, water and shelter. Passion is what drives an educator. It's internal and abstract, yet it drives us over and through multiple experiences while, keeping us committed to our craft over time. It wakes us up in the morning, and gives us zeal, so we may seek out chances to impact our students every chance we get. Passion delivers results! Compassion is more external and affective. It's something we give our students (care, empathy and charity) in the form of coaching, guidance and special accommodations that enable them to succeed while holding them accountable. Knowledge is familiarity, understanding or awareness of facts, information, or skills. Content knowledge can be described as specified knowledge that teachers teach and students are expected to learn; however, it's simply not enough to have knowledge of your craft without understanding the importance of being able to effectively disseminate that knowledge to your students. Knowledge has little meaning if it isn't combined with passion and compassion.

I see these three qualities displayed and intertwined cohesively in my teaching. First, knowledge can be described as the tip of the iceberg. What lies beneath, the how and why, is my passion and compassion. Without their working together, I could never effectively anchor and scaffold my students. They too, are part of the iceberg! We all see the tip, but my passion and compassion, through unwavering guidance, teaching and coaching has the fuel to motivate them to the top. There are many oppositional forces that inhibit passion, knowledge and compassion. Passion can be inhibited by fear, lack of commitment, disengagement, excuses and poor behavior. Knowledge can be inhibited by fear, teacher burnout, emotional and psychological illness and lack of support or resources. Compassion can be prohibited by anger, lack of knowledge, illness, self-centeredness, lack of tolerance, and lack of self -love/care.

Resources like this devotional book, Cortland's Grace to Teach blog and other colleagues, friends and family help in many ways. They are reminders that we are not alone. We have the people and resources we need, along with the word of God, to help us fulfill our passion. It is important for an educator to be committed to lifelong learning in professional practice as well as professional growth and development, because this "knowledge" will be used as a catalyst to fuel their passion in order to extend compassion, based on their student's needs. Technology, times, philosophies, and people change, so we must forever stretch our height and depth of knowledge. What better way to do so than doing something you love? Educating the world one student at a time! Besides teaching, being a daughter, wife, mother and friend contributes to my strength as an educator. Miraculously, somehow, I'm able to take those roles and find a way to apply my knowledge gained as an educator to being a daughter, wife, mother and friend. I can always extend Grace that I render, on a daily basis to my students, to my spouse, family and friends as well. Different groups of people and sets of circumstances, but the same three essential qualities: passion, knowledge and compassion. I balance being an educator with my roles outside of the profession through daily meditation and reflective practices, which enables me to assess what worked, what didn't work, and what needs to be improved upon.

My advice for a first-year teacher would be to find your passion. Whether it is general teaching or subject matter teaching and using the knowledge that you've attained to effectively and affectively impact your students, families and colleagues. When we highlight our strengths, our weaknesses tend to disappear. Take time out for self-care and daily reflections with that same knowledge, passion, and compassion that you extend to your students and families. In order to be effective, you must be well. An educator should not allow the principal or the school climate to drastically affect their impact in the classroom. Boundaries must be established early on to reduce the impact of outside influences. You were destined for greatness. Your students need something from you, and you need something from them! Take care of you first, so that you may use your passion- to fuel the knowledge you need, and to show compassion to every single student, every single day! Before they were born, God also knew that those students would need you to help influence the others that will come after them, and so on. God so loved the world, that He gave His only Son, so that whoever believes in Him shall not perish, but have eternal life. God is all-knowing, the Beginning and the End, the Alpha and the Omega...He's all knowledge. Jesus was his passion, and He had compassion for you so that you may be right where you are, right now... Reading this book! It has everything you need, and it was written by a true man of God! May each daily devotion, be the spark of joy to you, as it was to me each time I logged onto my page and found a post from Cortland Jones, waiting for me! Blessings!

Altamese Larkins, NBCT 2003

Contents

DAY 1: Introduction 1

DAY 2: Passion. 3

DAY 3: Knowledge 5

DAY 4: Compassion. 7

DAY 5: Inspiration. 9

DAY 6: Code of Conduct: The Lesson Plan for Discipline 11

DAY 7: Envisioning the Perfect Classroom. 13

DAY 8: Motivation. 15

DAY 9: Classroom Management. 17

DAY 10: Crumpled Paper. 19

DAY 11: Determination. 21

DAY 12: Student Learning Objectives. 23

DAY 13: Perspective Impacts Performance 27

DAY 14: Restoration: Insight about Teacher Burnout. 29

DAY 15: Life Long Learner 31

DAY 16: Consequences, Encouragement, and Maintenance 35

DAY 17: Refreshed. 37

DAY 18: Best Practices: Think Innovation 39

DAY 19: Culture Conducive for Learning 41

DAY 20: Revived: Coping with Teacher Burnout. 43

DAY 21: Making Connection between Content and Clientele 45

DAY 22: Empowerment- The Student's Role & Responsibility 47

DAY 23: Perseverance. 49

DAY 24: Rigor. 51

DAY 25: Promoting Self-Efficacy 53

DAY 26: Endurance 55

DAY 27: Interdisciplinary Approach 57

DAY 28: Making Allies out of Adversaries. 59

DAY 29: Manifestation Mindset. 61

DAY 30: Differentiating: Teaching to Their Intelligence 63

DAY 31: Community Requires Unity. 67

Dedication 71

Thank You Notes 73

DAY 1

Introduction

The first 3 years of my career as an educator sold me on the profession of being a classroom teacher. During the first 3 years my principal would arrange for staff members to go on a retreat paid for by the school district. During these staff retreats we would engage in team building activities and at other times we would participate in breakout sessions with other staff members from other school communities and school districts. It was these encounters and interactions that were the most memorable and rewarding to my early development as a professional. What I remember most from those encounters was hearing other professionals share their successes and challenges that allowed me to see I was not the only one experiencing the difficulties of teaching. In addition to this, it was an opportunity to learn from others' successes and strategies I could make use of to improve my professional practice. It was during these encounters of being on retreat I actually expressed out loud the sentiment of being sold on being a teacher if every school year would include such professional retreats. It literally felt like we were taking a vacation in the middle of the school year, and we would return refreshed, reinvigorated, and ready to take on those challenges armed and empowered to tackle difficulties faced as a classroom teacher.

Apples of Grace 31 Days of Inspiration for the Educator provides the opportunity for the classroom teacher to take a mental and emotional retreat from the reality of the challenges and difficulties associated with being an educator. Like the encounter of small group breakout sessions this book becomes a professional dialogue of insights, information, and inspiration to arm and empower you with motivation. You will be fueled to take on those challenges and tackle the difficulties you face daily within the classroom and your school community as you receive the apples of grace shared within these pages. Too often educators are viewed as the problem with what's wrong with the system of education. As the challenges mount, concerns grow on how to solve the problem, it is the educator who bears the brunt of the blame and the load of the responsibility to ensure no child is left behind. Overwhelmed and overworked, an educator who is passionate about his or her craft, knowledgeable about how to deliver their content in tangible ways that inspire learning, and who remains consistent in demonstrating compassion towards their students learns to excel and thrive. *Apples of Grace* becomes that resource by which the educator can stand firm in the face of the oppositional forces and the reality of "teacher burnout," and can resolve to be the change to make a difference in the lives of the children they instruct.

It is my sincere hope and prayer that readers of *Apples of Grace* will seek to use and reuse the content of this book to aid them in having the perspective and persistence fueled by the content to excel and thrive in their roles within the classroom. Like the inspiration that comes from professional dialogue that enhances professional practice, I hope this book creates that experience for its readers. The same enjoyment felt from the first 3 years of my career from those retreats, along with the 13 years served as a classroom management facilitator for managing student misbehavior, motivates me in sharing my experiences and expertise within the pages of this book. Having to return to the classroom in 2010, after 10 years outside of the classroom, I understand the difficulty associated with 'teacher burnout' in trying to remain optimistic and motivated, and I believe this book will be a great source of encouragement for the professional struggling in their role as an educator. Although some may not value the role of the educator as an honorable profession, I wrote this book to reaffirm my own belief in what I do in making a difference in the lives of children and I share the content of this book to honor those who believe they can, do, or aspire to make a difference. Enjoy the apples of grace received from the content shared within the pages of this book.

DAY 2

Passion

*"My food," said Jesus,
"is to do the will of him who sent me
and to finish his work."*

John 4:34

What is passion? How would you describe it? Why is it essential to being effective as an educator? I am reminded of Julie, a professional colleague I met in 2010. Reflecting on my understanding of passion, I recall watching how she pursued excellence as a classroom teacher. It was her first year as an educator. She was one of many new teachers who were a part of our staff in 2010-2011. Not only was it Julie's first year as a new teacher, but she was also making the transition into education by leaving a lucrative position as an attorney. She discovered a passion for wanting to serve as an educator, desiring to make a difference in the classroom, by preparing young minds for the future. It was something I had always heard about; people walking away from a field that was financially fulfilling to find fulfillment in an active role of service. Even more inspiring was watching Julie diligently work at her craft as a world language instructor teaching Spanish to middle school students within a community designated as a "turnaround" school.

Because ours was a "turnaround" school, most of our staff was made up of new to teaching, or first year teachers, with an entirely new administrative team. In the face of *great* student misconduct, in the midst of a turbulent, extremely stressful school environment, Julie persisted and persevered in demanding of herself and her students the excellence of teaching and learning. Despite the many oppositional forces and trying circumstances, several of Julie's students were recognized for high achievement in mastery of the Spanish language at the end-of-year eighth grade ceremony. Memorable, because the eighth graders were the most challenging group to work with that school year, making Julie's accomplishments with her eighth graders that much more significant.

> *"When people are caught up for that which is right and they are willing to sacrifice for it, there is no stopping point short of victory."*
> Rev. Dr. Martin Luther King, Jr., I've Been to the Mountaintop

Returning to the classroom in 2010, Julie modeled for me what passion in an educator looked like. A former attorney taught a world language class, helping rebellious middle-school students earn distinguished honors learning the Spanish language. At the conclusion of his memorable speech, Dr. King said it didn't matter what happened to him, because he had been to the mountaintop. The same "food" Jesus mentioned having, that Dr. King felt, I saw in Julie. I was inspired seeing her in action, because it challenged me to consider what I could do to have a similar outcome. Her determined disposition and deliberate resolve to be impactful motivated me. Take action, as an educator that inspires student achievement. Discover your "food" that fuels and moves you to promote excellence.

- *If life were like a video game, what would the meter read currently on your level of "passion" on a scale of 1-10?*

- *How does passion make a difference for the educator in the classroom and how does this influence the students?*

- *Who do you see, as an educator, that emulates being passionate about being an educator?*

DAY 3

Knowledge

"The function of education is to teach one to think intensively and to think critically. Intelligence plus character – that is the goal of true education."
Rev. Dr. Martin Luther King, Jr.

Mrs. Kaplan was a high school math teacher. Mr. Savoy was a high-school art teacher. The way they instructed changed my life. I remember Mrs. Kaplan for her persistence demanding of us to show how we arrived at our answer, like a drill sergeant. In my mind's eye I still see her seated at her overhead projector bellowing out, step by step, the procedure of mathematic equations. The room was dark, but for the light that illuminated from the projector surrounding Mrs. Kaplan's miniature stature as she thundered away, in demonstrating how she arrived at producing the correct formula.

As a visual learner, for the first time in my academic career, math finally made sense. After an arduous journey for me through early elementary and middle school, in high school I felt like Isaac Newton discovering the law of gravity. Mrs. Kaplan's demand to adhere to the discipline of solving mathematical equations through the use of visual repetition sparked within me the ability to feel empowered as a math student. I finished my academic career with a B average in high school, where I remembered earning E's in early elementary school and feeling inadequate in math during my academic career.

"Discipline is not the enemy of enthusiasm."
Morgan Freeman, Lean On Me

One day in art class Mr. Savoy told me that he only wanted me to draw only cartoon art, seeing it was what I enjoyed doing most. The timing of that directive spared me the unfavorable task of learning to work with clay on the dreaded wheel, but his words set me free and pointed me in the direction of what drove my passion to engage in creative self-expression.

That day of emancipation from toiling in the enslavement of clay led to my creating my own cartoon character, which was published in the high-school newspaper and selling t-shirts, and it fueled my aspiration to become a writer and illustrator of children's books. I taught cartoon art at two different community centers in Prince George's County Maryland and coordinated students to illustrate for authors within the community needing illustrators, in part, because of Mr. Savoy's directive to do cartoon art. In his return to coaching as head coach of the Washington Redskins, Mike Shanahan created a system that allowed Robert Griffin to excel as a rookie quarterback empowering him to earn rookie of the year honors and distinguished him in history as an NFL player. I admired and respected Coach Shanahan for making adjustments in how he coached to enable his quarterback to thrive. Effective teaching involves making adjustments. Take action in being persistent in reinforcing the discipline that inspires student self-efficacy in learning and consider how to integrate the student's interests in your instruction.

- *How can I reinforce the value of the discipline while still making learning fun?*

- *Is there a way I can differentiate instruction to my struggling learners allowing them to tap into making connection through their interests that inspires learning?*

- *Who do I know, as an educator, who excels in the use of differentiated instruction to help their students thrive?*

DAY 4

Compassion

"There are amazingly wonderful people in all walks of life; some familiar to us and others not. Stretch yourself and really get to know people. People are in many ways one of our greatest treasures."
Bryant H. McGill

Since 1979 I have been an avid Pittsburgh Steelers fan. When I first started watching football, the Pittsburgh Steelers were playing the Los Angeles Rams in the Super Bowl. The rest is history. I know for many of you this may be a difficult read if you are not a football fan, or you are a fan of another team, but you have my sympathy for not being a Steelers' fan.

"People think motivation comes from the mouth. Motivation comes from helping someone get the job done."
Chuck Noll, former Head Coach, Pittsburgh Steelers

From the moment of hearing this quote, viewing a documentary on the success of the team's accomplishments in winning their sixth Super Bowl title, it resonated with me. Chuck Noll's statement on motivation reinforced the need to recall my "why?" when looking to engage and enlist my students in the participation of classroom learning. Hearing those words on motivation from someone so distinguished and successful in their profession as Chuck Noll created a moment of pause and clarity for me. It challenged me to consider my perspective in my past use of motivation to engage my students in learning. Often, when you listen to the weekly pregame analytical dialogue from sports analysts and former athletes, there is consistent repetition of the fact that the most effective coaches are those who put their players in the best position to perform, succeed, and achieve. There are references and debates about the effectiveness of the "player's coach" versus the "autocratic leadership-style coach." As a child, all I remembered was how watching football made me feel. It was inspiring to see these magical, magnificent moments of competition between opposing teams, culminating in unbelievable, awe-inspiring, captivating encounters that, at times, were often gut-wrenching, debilitating, and exhilarating all at the same time. It was like riding a roller coaster.

As an adult, with the advent of technology and social media providing more extended coverage of so many aspects of the game of football, I find it intriguing to listen intensely to analytics involving the process of coaching that influences the team's performance on Sundays. So much so, over the past few years, I have come to liken my role as an educator to that of a 'professional coach.' My planning and preparation, as the classroom teacher, must be strategically synchronized with genuine consideration of how to translate the lesson in a way that allows my "team" of students to process the information, progress in learning, succeed, and achieve. Chuck Noll's quote about motivation takes on new meaning. Take action in planning how to demonstrate support in instruction that motivates student engagement in the process of learning and inspires them.

- *What are practical ways to motivate student engagement in the classroom without verbally demanding they be motivated to learn?*
- *How does preparedness and planning affect the teacher's and student's performance in the classroom?*
- *Besides the dissemination of the lesson, what else should I plan and prepare for as the "coach" of my "team" of students?*

DAY 5

Inspiration

"Determination gives you the resolve to keep going in spite of the roadblocks that lay before you."
Dennis Waitley

During an intensely heated discussion about ways to influence change in student misconduct at a classroom-management seminar, there was a strong sense that some ideas were not being received openly. The prevailing thought amongst the participants - classroom teachers from elementary, middle, and high school - was that the proposed strategies appeared to be appropriate for elementary-age students, but not so much for high-school students. I remember that the setting was somewhat overcrowded and that the temperature was somewhat uncomfortable. The rising tension of resistance to the information being presented didn't help. Though the feelings of frustration from the push back of the evening's content was not unfamiliar, the intensity of emotion I felt driving home motivated the challenge of how to reinforce the principles and strategies despite the momentary opposition to the content. In the moment of driving home, clarity and inspiration illuminated the thought of how to convey the principle of redirecting oppositional, or adversarial, behavior displayed by students.

"Let us rise up tonight with a greater readiness. Let us stand with a greater determination. Let us move on in these powerful days of challenge to make America what it ought to be. We have the opportunity to make America a better nation."
Rev. Dr. Martin Luther King, Jr.

What came to me was to share how one man's persistence in expressing his belief in the ideals of humanity and a nation united, despite the great adversity, opposition, and intolerance faced, enabled him to influence change in our *nation*. How much more, then, can one educator, inspired and determined to affect positive change, be influential in motivating oppositional, adversarial students to become allies within the *classroom* setting.

The insight and inspiration received from that clarity of recalling the challenge Dr. King faced in seeking to affect positive change within our nation was an epiphany that helped to shift the atmosphere of the workshop. The participants were empowered in being open-minded to considering more how they could make a difference with individuals and circumstances that seemed overwhelming, or impossible to affect change. The lesson learned is in the realization that the desired change I look for in my students has to begin with me. The moment of clarity received and imparted to the workshop participants enabled them to see that what had appeared to be impossible could be possible with a change in perspective and strategy. All of this occurred because of the *inspiration* received from a desire to empower the workshop participants to believe in what's possible. Take action to look beyond the momentary challenges and oppositional behaviors to bridge your student's limitations to a new way of thinking that equips, enables, and empowers them to achieve and thrive.

- *Where do you draw inspiration from to motivate you during challenging times faced in your role as an educator?*

- *What is one current circumstance, or individual, that presents a challenge and what steps can be taken to begin making progress towards affecting positive change?*

- *How could journaling be beneficial to building and sustaining a momentum of inspiration to carry you through the school year?*

DAY 6

Code of Conduct: The Lesson Plan for Discipline

"When a country is rebellious, it has many rulers, but a ruler with discernment and knowledge maintains order."
Proverbs 28:2 NIV

Does the *"immaculate lesson plan"* deter, dissuade, or discourage student misconduct from occurring? Shouldn't my proverbial soapbox soliloquy of passionately expressed expectations be enough to inspire and motivate students to behave? Overhearing a conversation between two students, one mentioned to the other their perspective that one of their teacher's persistent yelling made the teacher seem ineffective and incapable of managing their class.

That same school year a conversation with one of my students led me to share, "You should not train yourself as a student to only respond when someone is yelling at you. The only two places I am aware of where yelling is an acceptable form of communication are prison and the armed forces." I only wish I could have had that wisdom and insight during my third year as an educator. Anger, pride in being right, argumentative, and yelling were my tools of choice and the means by which I sought to manage my students and my classroom. I even broke a few yardsticks that year. A period I am still remorseful and grieved to know I conducted myself that way. I have since transitioned away from such actions. It was during my second year returning to the classroom, in my second school community in as many years, when a professional classroom colleague said to me, "As I watched you interact with the students, I thought you were crazy thinking the way you were seeking to engage the students in managing their behavior would not work and prove to be ineffective. Since then, I have come to admire the way you *manage yourself* working with the students and it helps me to see how what you do with the students, I could use to help me in dealing with some of the adults." Unknowingly to my colleague, those timely words of affirmation were like arriving at an oasis in the desert after an arduous, grueling journey enduring the intensity of heated emotion and push back of oppositional student behavior.

That moment came a year after talking with the classroom student about not being trained by a "raised voice." Receiving the compliment from my colleague made all that I had endured up to that moment worth the struggle. Like a heavyweight boxer, despite the barrage of direct blows, like anvils falling on the head of the countless cartoon characters watched as a child growing up, I was able to rope-a-dope for 15 rounds, like Muhammad Ali, until the final bell. Effective teaching requires planning for student misconduct as a teacher plans his or her daily classroom lesson. Order in the classroom begins with a strategic plan of how order will be established by the classroom teacher. Take action in considering preparation for moments of student misconduct during classroom instruction.

- *What are 3-5 behaviors, or classroom expectations, that you and your students can exemplify to create a positive environment?*

- *What strategies can be employed to correct misbehavior, encourage appropriate behavior, motivate consistent behavior?*

- *Why is it important to display, reinforce, reteach, and refer back to classroom expectations, or include as part of a lesson?*

DAY 7

Envisioning the Perfect Classroom

"It's the teacher that makes the difference, not the classroom."
Michael Morpurgo

Is it possible to find the ideal classroom? Does an educator ever consider the role he or she plays in creating the ideal classroom environment, or resign to thinking that students should just come in, sit down, and engage in learning without any direction, or facilitation? Just as it is the desire of the educator for the student to take ownership of their role and responsibility in contributing positively to the classroom environment, so must the teacher lead and model in his or her own role and responsibility.

Think about this. There is a select group of students that, no matter what, enter the classroom, are prepared, and consistently engage without little direction. There are even classrooms like this where a majority of the students demonstrate exemplary self-efficacy skills. Then there is a larger group of students who function better with clear, concise direction and understood expectations for daily rituals and routines. For such students, depending on the day, whether they have eaten, if they are on speaking terms with their friends, or they actually like you today, will determine how successful they will be in performing and producing the quality of work required. Lastly, there is a small, but infamous group of students who seem to be strategically placed in almost every classroom across America whose sole purpose, it seems, is to operate in opposition to everything from procedures, to expectations, to contributing positively to the classroom environment. Usually, this group numbers two-three students, but if I am unsuccessful in learning to make them allies and only regard them

13

as adversaries they can create havoc and cause a lot of damage. There are classrooms that can be identified with what I like to call *'classroom personalities,'* just as these personalities can be identified within individual students. Does the ideal environment include students who consistently manage their own behavior which includes accepting the consequences of their behavior in an ideal classroom setting?

Is it realistic to envision the ideal classroom absent of misconduct? My reflection upon the visualization of the ideal classroom brings to mind the idea of the music conductor. An orchestra is made up of various musical instruments, each with its unique, distinct sound. At times, a classroom can sound like an orchestra playing without its conductor. Out of rhythm, out of sync, out of tune, the sound of the classroom can be an awful array of screeching stringed instruments, blaring horns sounding like an elephant sneezing, and a clutter of wind and brass piercing the ears and senses like fingernails scraping a chalkboard. An orchestra member is responsible for playing 'in tune.' The student must learn to engage cooperatively. The educator's challenge is conducting in a way that inspires student accountability. Like the maestro, resolve to instruct in a manner that unites unique, distinct individuals in the process of learning producing a harmonic symphony and atmosphere conducive for learning.

- *How much does an educator's perception affect his or her ability to inspire and influence students to engage and cooperate?*

- *Do all students have the ability to demonstrate appropriate classroom behavior? If no, why? If yes, then consider if you may be expecting less from an individual student, or class and how to move them towards doing/being better.*

- *Do you think it's an educator's responsibility to motivate students to engage and participate in class? Why or why not?*

DAY 8

Motivation

"When the Celtics and the Lakers played in the 2008 Finals, those were the greatest times of my life, those battles with Magic and the Lakers. We fought like hell for the same thing for over 12 years, and through it all, the respect was always there."

Larry Bird

To perform at your peak level as an educator, are you driven internally, or externally? At the time of writing, I am reading *When the Game Was Ours* by Larry Bird and Earvin Magic Johnson with Jackie MacMullan. The book is a personal account, from Bird and Johnson's perspective, of their migration from college into the NBA. Their impact on the evolution of the game of basketball was inspired by their decade long struggle for supremacy, competing in leading their respective teams towards the ultimate goal of winning NBA championships. They candidly share their mutual respect, competitive jealousy, and how they influenced each other's personal ambition to be better and do better in order to outdo the other in their journey from college into the pros. Remembering my love for the game of basketball, being introduced to it through watching Magic Johnson on television as a teenager, I can relate to Larry Bird's quote of his great memories recalled from his duels with Magic. Their mutual respect and admitted jealousy of each other's athletic prowess in how it motivated the two of them to perform at their best in order to out-duel each other provides the perfect tone for this reflection on the subject of motivation.

A recent conversation had with a college graduate, the same day I bought the book and 2 days before writing this content on motivation included their expressed discontentment with her supervisor's inability to lead in a way that inspires. She shared their frustration in how the lack of leadership was fueling a growing climate of disgruntled, unenthusiastic colleagues and how it was affecting my friend's ability to feel fulfilled at work. The first year I began teaching, it was my ambition to put my school community on the map with regard to art. Within that year, 3 of my students were honored with recognition for their drug awareness posters and I was nominated for a first-year teacher's award.

Is it possible to thrive in an environment that doesn't fuel you? Returning to the classroom in 2010, I mentioned my colleague Julie whose inspiring initiative as a former attorney turned educator, during her first year, motivated me as I watched her engage her students in excelling and being honored in learning Spanish. Today, I have a colleague whom I admire who instructs her orchestra in a manner that leads to them earning awards and recognition from the county. It was these two colleagues, along with my deliberate intention to recapture my "why?" in being an educator who aided my transition returning to the classroom. Be determined to maintain and regain momentum in your effort to excel and thrive as an educator.

- *What motivates you more to excel, wanting to excel, or your student's performance from your instruction?*
- *How much does, or should the principal influence or impact my ability to excel, or perform?*
- *Who is someone you know as an educator who inspires you to excel? Why?*

DAY 9

Classroom Management

"Better a patient person than a warrior, one with self-control than one who takes a city."
Proverbs 16:32 NIV

What does 'effective classroom management' look like? Is it managing a classroom where everyone is seated, settled, and silent? In reflecting upon classroom management, do you envision a classroom where the teacher is in control, domineering, and leads by being an authoritarian? Is it visualized as the teacher being an authoritative facilitator where students are in control of themselves, and both adult and children are working together collaboratively in a process of learning? When thinking about the scope of what classroom management entails, should consideration be given to the probability and potential for student misconduct to occur in devising a lesson plan?

Just as one considers consequences for misconduct in redirecting a student to engage, is it possible that inclusion of recognition and reward strategies or incentives may help influence student engagement and participation? Have you ever employed the strategy of turning off the lights, movement, or rearranging of student desks, change of voice, or inclusion of students in assisting with classroom tasks as part of classroom management? What about enlisting students as aids, peer tutors, interpreters, or designating days when they lead instruction? Would allowing them to have "voice," or say in procedures, expectations, or input to special activities for themselves, or as a group, be considered a part of classroom management? Is classroom management solely about the room, the students, me as the educator, or all-inclusive? Do you think there is a difference between looking to punish a student for misconduct instead of disciplining the student?

Ultimately, a punishment invokes the perspective of "what I do to the child." However, if discipline means to teach, then a fresh perspective requires me to consider what I will do "with the child" to help them be and do better. Is punishment for misconduct the only means by which this occurs? Effective classroom management requires consequences for inappropriate behavior. This aids students to employ self-correcting behaviors and being responsive to redirection to cooperate.

Does "effective classroom management" mean there's no disruption caused by student misbehavior? Before I make demands that my students display self-control, am I modeling it in how I communicate, employ correction strategies, and engage misbehaving students in order to redirect them? Posted in my classroom the first 9 years of my career were the expectations: focus, effort, patience, and responsibility. When I returned to the classroom, I added diligence and perseverance. At the beginning of every school year, each new semester, and embedded within each unit taught, I have learned to explain to my students daily the need for them to practice these principles. I remind them that successful productivity in their artwork, in helping me to consistently experience the type of classroom environment conducive to being creative, begins and ends with their initiative to employ these principles. Embed strategies, within your lesson, to reinforce desired behaviors and discipline for correction and redirection.

- *How can you encourage students to take ownership of their responsibility to participate in learning?*
- *Can I make students do anything, or do they choose to, or not to comply?*
- *Why does remaining calm in the midst of disorder, long term, have a greater impact in influencing student behavior?*

DAY 10

Crumpled Paper

"When he saw the crowds, he had compassion on them, because they were harassed and helpless, like sheep without a shepherd."

Matthew 9:36 NIV

During a heated debate with my colleague and the staff of an alternative school community involving whether proposed classroom management principles for the type of students they were accustomed to working with; an idea came to me involving a sheet of clean notebook paper. Sensing the opportunity to reenter the intensely debated dialogue, I calmly invited everyone to consider the clean sheet of unmarred notebook paper I held in my hand. Sensing the wave of silence that fell over the group, I began explaining what I understood as the heart of the matter in the hidden message behind the appearance of resistance to the content presented. We desire our students to be that clean sheet of unmarred notebook paper as they assemble in our classroom. In our hearts and minds, we imagine the ideal of prepared, engaged, enthusiastic learners who willingly participate without displaying resistant, oppositional behavior.

Then I balled up that clean sheet of unmarred notebook paper and slowly began to unravel it. I placed it on the table nearby seeking to flatten and smooth it out to help it return to its original state. In doing this, I held up the paper again calmly explaining the reality of what we encounter in spite of the ideal desires we have in our mind. We're expecting our students, who represent the *crumpled paper* to be like that unmarred, crisp sheet of notebook paper I originally held up. Instead of entering our classrooms eager, enthusiastic, prepared, and engaged, they are disengaged, distracted, disruptive, dysfunctional, disrespectful, disobedient…..crumpled paper! *Aaaaagggghhhhh!*

I recall a young man whom I would address with the title "Mister". A practice I still do. One day he asked why I called him "Mister," he felt he was not important to be regarded as such. Although he felt like crumpled paper, I wanted him to know I saw him as a clean sheet. Surprised that he didn't think himself to be important enough to be regarded that way, I simply told him that he was someone deserving of my respect. Every new school year brings new challenges and new students, but for the most part the behaviors are the same. We see new faces when school reopens, but the same old behaviors emerge. It's like shopping for new school supplies, but purchasing neatly wrapped, used notebook paper. Seeing our students as *crumpled paper*, we begin to regard and treat them like crumpled paper. We see them as less valuable, unworthy of our time and energy, so we are less motivated to engage in the effort of smoothing out the crinkles. Through acceptance, with the proper perspective, empower students to maximize the full potential of who they can be, like clean paper, so they can thrive in the classroom.

- *Why is our perspective of our students important in our role as educators?*

- *Do you recall a time when your perspective, negative or positive, had an impact? What was the outcome?*

- *Identify a student, or students, whom you see as crumpled paper and consider steps to take to work differently to produce different, positive outcomes for you and the student.*

DAY 11

Determination

"A dream doesn't become reality through magic; it takes sweat, determination and hard work."
Colin Powell

Is your heart fueled with ambition to excel in your craft, inspiring your students to achieve, in a way distinguishes you in what you do in influencing student performance? In my inquiry I am not asking about awards and recognition so much as I am leading you to consider what drives you to strive. There is a quote that resonates that simply states; *"Always allow your reach to exceed your grasp."*

Wanting more out of my students requires something of me. What am I willing to invest of myself to see the desired return in my students? Is this demanded consistently? By the conclusion of my third year of teaching, I was not heading in the direction I aspired to go in to become the educator I had in my mind to be. Over the summer of '95, I registered for a classroom management workshop that proved to be the motivational spark I needed to help me move away from using angry, argumentative, punitive strategies to motivate student cooperation and engagement. During my fourth year, I worked on controlling my anger and reminding students of their responsibility to choose appropriate behavior - or accept the consequences of inappropriate choices without engaging in arguments. I shared my new strategies and lessons learned from the summer, throughout my fourth year, with my colleague across the hall who had more than 30 years of experience. By the end of my fourth year, to my surprise, my colleague was retiring and cited my sharing in what helped her to encounter, in her words, her best year as an educator. It was fulfilling and rewarding, as a fourth-year teacher, to know something I had shared benefitted a seasoned veteran of the profession. It also sold me on the understanding what I had learned over the summer of '95 was helpful and practical for anyone to benefit from regardless of years of experience. By my sixth year I was trained to facilitate the very workshops I participated in and had learned from.

Beyond envisioning the ideal classroom, does your mind's eye dream about who you aspire to be as an educator? During my ninth year I felt like I was becoming the classroom teacher I aspired to be. I was learning how to work with and influence perceived adversaries into classroom allies. Great at punishing students I didn't like, or get along with, I was now learning how to discipline, or work with despite oppositional behavior. This was achieved by learning how to separate my feelings, the misbehavior, and the student from one another and encourage the student to manage the behavior while I managed my feelings. I found more students, over time, accepting consequences for misbehavior, less arguments, and increased cooperation. Be determined to employ best practices in your role as an educator that equips you to empower your students.

- *Why is it important to make self-reflection, inventory or assessment, a consistent part of your process and journey in being an educator?*

- *How does staying informed of professional best practices contribute to your overall effectiveness as a classroom teacher?*

- *Do you recall a victorious classroom moment you successfully influenced a perceived adversary into becoming an ally? Consider what was done to achieve that success and replicate it with other students.*

DAY 12

Student Learning Objectives

"Being busy does not always mean real work. The object of all work is production or accomplishment and to either of these ends there must be forethought, system, planning, intelligence, and honest purpose, as well as perspiration. Seeming to do is not doing."

Thomas A. Edison

"If properly implemented, student learning objectives help teachers bring more science to their art, strengthen instructional support to the classrooms, and improve the quality of the outcome."

William J. Slotnik, *Founder & CEO of Community Training and Assistance Center*

The day I planned to write the content of student learning objectives, I had a conversation with my son about a mentoring meeting he had involving the topic of accountability, responsibility, and maturity. Before that conversation, he had notified me he was unsuccessful, as an incoming freshman, in making the high-school basketball team. My son felt confident he would succeed next year, because of the support he has from his network of friends, as well as his cousin, who played on the collegiate level, whom I asked to mentor and coach my son. Despite falling short of his goal, my son believed these two supporters helped him feel confident about trying out, and that fuels his motivation for next year. Originally created, by Denver Public

Schools in 1999, as a means to link teacher pay to student outcomes, the student learning objective (SLO) is considered an effective tool by which educators can improve their instructional practices using ambitious focused targets that are appropriate and achievable. Content for this writing was influenced by a document published by the Reform Support Network that explains, *"Like well-constructed SLO's, good instruction includes gathering data, setting goals based on data, and then assessing whether the goals have been met."* The basic premise of the SLO is to improve student performance by gathering data from student performance in order to influence progress towards growth in student achievement with a targeted learning goal. The teacher identifies specific goals according to data gathered from student performance to enhance instruction and student learning outcomes.

An effective SLO includes:
   a) targeted student population,
   b) time period,
   c) assessments of student progress,
   d) rigorous, realistic expectations for student growth,
   e) strong rationale, and f) effective strategies for
      achieving SLO goals.

The Reform Support Network document cited *"good instructional practice"* and *"helpful in influencing educators to buy in to state and district evaluation systems"* as two benefits of student learning objectives. During our conversation about the mentoring meeting, I asked my son to describe his understanding of accountability. He mentioned that it relates to owning what he needs to do. I added his citing his friends and cousin as a "support" to his initiative to play basketball. I reiterated from the mentoring topic, that personal *accountability* to one's goals is *responsibility* in action and the demonstration of *maturity*. Arm yourself with the latest best practices to empower you to excel in your instructional practice and help students achieve.

- *What 'supports' do you have in place that provide accountability to challenge you to excel in your craft?*

- *Do you see the SLO as a help, or hindrance, to your role and responsibility as an instructional leader in the classroom?*

- *If I remain resistant, defiant, and oppositional to instructional best practices is that a reflection on my maturity as a professional?*

DAY 13

Perspective Impacts Performance

"Everything we hear is an opinion, not a fact. Everything we see is a perspective, not the truth."
Marcus Aurelis

How important is it to believe every child has the ability to contribute positively and be productive? Transparency in storytelling became an effective tool in presenting effective classroom management strategies to empower workshop participants and encourage them in understanding they weren't the only ones who struggled with managing student misconduct.

"Mr. Jones can I help you pass those out?"

"No, thank you." I would reply. Every time this young man would ask, the reply was the same. Early in my career, fear of losing control of the classroom prompted me to require everyone to remain seated and wait to begin working until I had passed out all of the materials. Every time this particular student would ask to help, I would politely decline.

One day I made a courageous decision, after repeated attempts by the student to assist me, to pull the student aside and apologize. "I want to apologize to you, because I realize I was judging you, believing you would take advantage of the opportunity to help and use it to disrupt my class. I apologize for judging you as someone who would disrupt my class." The young man accepted my apology, and today, I have students helping me to do a lot of things. Even if they create, or cause disruption, I have learned to use it as a teachable moment. In that moment early in my career though, it was *my perception* that hindered me from allowing my students and me to experience something more than me trying to exert energy to control my students and limit their movement fueled by my own fears. Fear of losing control caused me to be restrictive, judgmental, critical, and controlling and created an atmosphere of limitation, opposition, and separation between my students and me. The young man perceived me as, possibly, needing help, whereas, I perceived him as a hindrance.

Can an educator perform optimally without optimism? Realistically and logically, I cannot hope to achieve the ideals of best instructional practices and achieve growth in student performance with a mindset that is confining and restrictive and inhibits my students and me from consistently performing at maximum potential. Courageous, honest introspection allowed me to confront myself and challenge the thoughts and emotions causing self-sabotage in my role as an educator. How can I consistently position my students to progress and succeed with a "restrictive" mindset? *"When you wake up every day, you have two choices. You can either be positive or negative; an optimist or a pessimist. I choose to be an optimist. It's all a matter of perspective."* - Harvey Mackay

How effective am I as an educator, really, if I can instruct only the "good kids?" Challenge yourself, and your students, to change thinking that limits, restricts, and confines that allows them to learn and thrive.

- *How much should I allow environmental factors, other's opinions, personal beliefs to influence my expectations in a student's ability to perform in my classroom?*

- *If I don't believe a child can succeed, then is it the child, or I, who limits his or her potential?*

- *What resources and supports can help me have a healthy, fresh perspective that empowers me and inspires my students?*

DAY 14

Restoration: Insight about Teacher Burnout

"Create in me a pure heart, O God, and renew a steadfast spirit within me. Restore to me the joy of your salvation and grant me a willing spirit, to sustain me."
Psalm 51:10, 12 NIV

How would you define *"teacher burnout?"* One colleague defined it as:

"Burnout means waking up each morning believing no matter how well I prepare or carry out instruction, the result will be less than the students need. There are simply too many factors contributing to the success or failure of student performance that are beyond the control of a classroom teacher. This realization leads to a feeling of hopelessness and helplessness.' Another colleague added, 'Period(s) within a school year, teachers feel unmotivated to teach, uninspired, no 'vibe' in relationship with students. The teacher produces uninspired lesson plans and students are less motivated to engage."

Like the great sense of peril felt in the dream of the continuous "freefall," or the horrifying powerlessness at the onset of the panic associated with drowning, the description of burnout depicted paints a vivid image of powerlessness from being overwhelmed, empty, or incapacitated.

In preparation of gathering data to draft the content for this topic, from the articles read and warning signs cited I was awakened in my consciousness to the reality I was encountering my own feelings of 'teacher burnout.' For the first time in my professional career I felt an overwhelming sense of being 'alone' in my role as an educator, feeling unsupported in my concerns within the community I was loyal to serve, a gnawing 'rubber band ball of frustration' was carried over from one school year into the start of a new school year. A first for me to end a year frustrated and start a new school year feeling frustrated. Researching content for *Restoration* became my 'life preserver' to save me from my awakened consciousness of drowning in my personal burnout from frustration. In my interview with Mrs. Brauer, a middle school World Language teacher, she felt that the feelings are probably unavoidable, but one can employ counter measures to offset the long term negative effects associated with teacher burnout.

Can I prevent myself from encountering 'teacher burnout, feeling overwhelmed, powerless, or incapacitated? One such strategy Mrs. Brauer offered of which I liked how she described it as the 'feel good' file of successes, notes, cards, keepsakes received to pull out and use to refuel yourself to get going again like a veteran boxer getting his final second pep talk before they arise from their corner to keep fighting the good fight. My other colleague mentioned, *"I would have been far better off spending more time away from work and expanding other interests."* Mrs. Brauer also noted the value of talking with respected colleagues and loved ones who can cheer you on, encourage you, and help keep you motivated. Balance your role as an educator with a lifestyle that refuels you.

- *Does acceptance of my limitations to affect change mean I am not passionate, motivated, concerned about helping my students?*

- *What should I do with the feelings associated with circumstances affecting my students that are beyond my ability to control?*

- *Can students experience "burnout" like teachers do? If yes, how can you help your students overcome feeling overwhelmed, or powerless?*

DAY 15

Life Long Learner

"Tell me and I forget. Teach me and I remember. Involve me and I learn."
Benjamin Franklin

Does life-long learning pertain to my ongoing personal academic enrichment, or can it be inclusive of my adaptability to the evolution of the classroom environment from past to present and future?

Complete this statement: The principle critical to my effectiveness in instruction regardless of the students I teach is . . . .

Understanding the real challenges classroom teachers face in delivering instruction in today's classroom environment, being **innovative** is the essential principle that helps with daily teaching and learning.

"A good teacher can inspire hope, ignite the imagination, and instill a love of learning."
Brad Henry

The challenge of the educator amid a myriad of distractions within the classroom and pressures outside the schoolhouse, is to be consistent and persistent in delivering daily instruction that promotes student engagement and facilitates enthusiasm in learning. The educator who exemplifies the nature of a lifelong learner makes personal inquiry daily on ways to deliver quality instruction that facilitates the process of learning with their students in a way that is fun and relevant and that promotes demonstration of student self-efficacy. How can I make use of real world experiences/current events/history/technology in my daily instruction to make it relevant and relatable to my students? On two separate occasions during my professional career coursework studied at Trinity University in Washington, DC was used to aid me in my role inside and outside of the classroom. In my early years as an art educator, taking a summer course in painting and the study of artist Vincent van Gogh's paintings of sunflowers inspired me to teach my students what I had learned from the workshop. During my pursuit of my Master's Degree for Counseling, I made immediate use of what was learned, from the subject of self-concept development, that allowed me to position high-school students to develop leadership skills and learn to become positive contributors to their school community.

What best practices, currently, can I integrate into my daily instruction that can enhance my performance and productivity of my students? Breaking the 'cycle of insanity' in expecting different results from my students by doing what is not working to get them to engage requires change in me to see change in them. To do this requires a breakthrough from the internal noise and external clamor of resignation, cynicism, and resistance to change. Some benefits of translating my love of lifelong learning to my role as an educator includes the fact that it:

    1) stimulates creative self-expression for teacher/student,

    2) helps generate innovative problem solving in students/ delivery of instruction,

    3) increases student engagement,

    4) influences student decision making,

    5) invites collaboration between teacher/student,

    6) creates an environment of empowerment for teacher/ student

    7) increases enthusiasm for instruction and learning,

    8) makes learning fun,

    9) promotes adherence to procedures and expectations, and

    10) instills ownership of student self-efficacy for learning and character development.

Facilitate a love of learning through innovation.

- *What is my core goal in teaching my students? What do I most want them to gain from my instruction?*

- *What is my main priority, or responsibility in my role as an educator in the classroom?*

- *Are there any students I teach who exemplify behaviors, or actions in how they engage, or produce work I can use to help facilitate instruction and learning?*

DAY 16

Consequences, Encouragement, and Maintenance

"What is necessary to change a person is to change his awareness of himself."
Abraham Maslow

Is there a distinction between punishment involving *doing something to a student* for misconduct and discipline involving *doing something with the student* to influence change in misbehavior? How would you describe the distinction between punitive consequences and restorative practices for student misbehavior?

If discipline means to teach, then at the core of *consequences* for misbehavior my goal should be to instruct the child in a way that inspires him or her to take ownership of his or her behavior, including accountability to accept the consequences of misbehavior. Learning to plan for and anticipate misbehavior as one plans for the daily instruction allows one to be better prepared for redirecting and influencing student choices towards consistently being positive, productive contributors to the classroom environment. After 24 years of teaching, the faces of the students change, but the behaviors of throwing paper, chewing gum, incessant talking, refusing to comply, coming unprepared, and having a litany of excuses for why the homework wasn't completed have not changed. Being proactive to create strategies and follow through consistently to hold my students accountable when these behaviors manifest allows me to feel empowered and empower my students to take responsibility for the various and variety of circumstances that can erupt within a classroom setting.

As Batman was equipped with a utility belt with multifaceted tools enabling him to escape any harrowing circumstance, educators can be equipped with sound, practical strategies that can aid them in effectively managing student misbehavior and in avoiding combative behaviors that escalate and disrupt instruction. For the past 2 school years (2015-2017), I deliberately chose to use encouragement and maintenance strategies on the classes I dreaded. That feeling you get when that 'group' of students come to your classroom that, like the weather, changes the atmosphere of your mood from clear skies to hurricane warning. Doing this over time, I learned to enjoy and look forward to seeing those students come into my room.

What is the purpose, or goal, of correcting a student's misbehavior? Encouragement strategies involve actions, or behaviors I demonstrate that causes students to feel valued, appreciated, or welcomed. Like **"catch 'em at the door."** A greeting at the door, as the students enter, to facilitate positive interaction between myself and each student to break the ice. *Maintenance* strategies involve recognition and reward strategies, associated with specific student actions and behaviors, that allow students to feel accepted and affirmed in being positive, productive contributors to the classroom community. Like putting names on the board of students who are doing the right thing instead of always acknowledging students who do the wrong thing. The practice of encouragement and maintenance strategies, along with consequences, provides insurance in limiting the amount of student misbehavior that occurs from day to day and safeguards both the student and teacher consistently from engaging in the oppositional behaviors. Strive to practice discipline that consistently turns student adversaries into allies.

- *The moment misbehavior occurs, does a consequence need to be enforced?*

- *Why does reliance upon the main office, or administrators, solely prove to be ineffective in managing a student's behavior?*

- *How can recognition strategies and rewards, or incentives, be used to motivate student engagement?*

DAY 17

Refreshed

"A generous person will prosper; whoever refreshes others will be refreshed."
Proverbs 11:25 NIV

When you think of the word *refreshed*, do these following meanings come to mind?

1) to give new strength, or energy to,
2) fortify,
3) revise or update (skills or knowledge), or
4) stimulate memory by going over previous information?

It was refreshing to see these various meanings and their relationship applicable to the context of teaching. In any school year, there is a natural weariness that takes place during the normalcy of routine with teaching and learning. Along with the need for a physical break that allows for rest from the demand of the routine of work for teachers and students, consider including strategies that promote being refreshed. Is there a "consequence" to the process of teaching and learning when students don't have opportunity for assemblies, social interaction during classroom instruction, or are expected to 'always' be instruction minded? Should the classroom teacher be considerately incorporate a "break in the routine" for their students? What happens to a classroom teacher who never socializes at work, has no break from the routine of instruction, can't discuss best practices with colleagues, or is not allowed to incorporate any creativity into facilitation of curriculum? My mind is not always on teaching when I am in the classroom and my students are not always thinking about learning. In the 10 years served outside the classroom, I spent time in conversation with students who were emotionally and mentally troubled by circumstances involving sexual abuse, domestic violence, low self-esteem, homelessness, bullying, thoughts of suicide, self-mutilation, identity crisis, feelings of neglect, abandonment, family issues associated with separation, divorce, running away from home, hunger, etc. One such child I met intentionally decided to stop performing academically in order to manipulate where she would live, no longer desiring to be with one parent because of impending divorce. How can a teacher help a child who is determined to not excel academically?

What is the benefit to taking inventory of where the children are mentally before instruction begins? All students may not desire to share, but what does being given the opportunity to speak communicate to a student? Can our "proverbial soapbox" moments be used to share an encouragement rather than just our complaints? If the entire class period does not require daily instruction from beginning to end consider a periodic "moment of reflection" that allows for the students to channel their thoughts in a creative way that facilitates self-expression. How can your love of sports, books, movies, travel, family, or other common interests with students be used to promote being refreshed? Plan and prepare for a special time of year – or throughout the year – for minimal breaks in routine to promote being refreshed in the classroom.

- *What do you do to give yourself a break from the routine and the demands of being an educator?*

- *Do you look ahead to that time of year (usually March) where there are no breaks in routine to plan opportunities for you and your students to be refreshed?*

- *How can I employ my students to aid me in promoting "brain breaks," or being refreshed that increases productivity and enthusiasm for learning?*

DAY 18

Best Practices: Think Innovation

"For good ideas and true innovation, you need human interaction, conflict, argument, debate."
Margaret Heffernan

What is the simplest, most effective resource to inspire innovation? My graphic design class composed of sixth and seventh grade students, in 2015, were invited through inquiry to think of ways to create opportunities for student service for the peers of their school community. The students willing to help generate ideas formed a student committee and two students within the committee came forward with aspirations to establish a student-led leadership training program that would operate during the summer as a summer camp program.

The simplest effective resource to spark and inspire innovation is inquiry, or the proposal of questions/problems to elicit responses for resolution, or solutions. Regarding 'best practices,' what is at the heart of innovation, or why should I strive to be innovative as an educator? What does innovation look like within classroom instruction? Along with classroom instruction, what are other ways innovation can be applied to the classroom environment?

Simply stated innovation is defined as a new method, idea, or product. Other words related are revolution, change, alteration, transformation, metamorphosis, breakthrough, inspiration, or creativity to mention a few. Does all innovation have to be facilitated by the educator during instruction? Inspired by the inquiry to generate ideas for student service opportunities for the students of their school community, two programs have been implemented and currently operate since the committee was established in spring of 2015. Before and after school, students earn student service hours by visiting the local elementary school to read to

39

and tutor K-3 students to promote and celebrate literacy. For a brief time, students stayed after school to earn student service hours by assisting the evening custodial staff in cleaning up the school community by emptying the trash, wiping down windows, and vacuuming. These students contributed creative ideas that inspired positive change within their school community, leading to products offering a service to the local elementary school and opportunity for students to earn student service hours. The two students looking to create the student-led leadership training program are now in high school, but their program continues to operate with students visiting the local elementary school to teach leadership and responsibility to K-3 students.

What are the opponents to innovation? How can we teach children to identify and overcome the internal/external opponents to innovation? Dialogue with my students about building and sustaining momentum in contributing consistently to class and work led a student to discuss the subject of inertia as the threat to momentum. One day in class another student simply stated, "Mr. Jones, I feel like I am experiencing inertia," to describe loss of momentum in doing his work. Within the last school year, the two students creating the student-led program grew to five students, and we talked in class because of their inquiry one day about how to overcome procrastination. Promote innovation in your classroom through inquiry.

- *What internal/external threats oppose a teacher's desire to promote inquiry and innovation?*

- *Five tips to promote innovation cited by KQED News include:*
  1) infuse passion into learning (student interests),
  2) try something new,
  3) consider the 'flipped classroom model,'
  4) tap into student's ideas, and
  5) incorporate discovery.

- *Which of the 5 do you do and which one would you consider doing?*

Steve Jobs has stated, "Innovation distinguishes between a leader and a follower." Do you agree or disagree? Can innovation strategies be used to influence challenging students to engage and cooperate more?

DAY 19

Culture Conducive for Learning

"It is the supreme art of the teacher to awaken joy in creative expression and knowledge."
Albert Einstein

What components make a classroom environment conducive for learning? In the writing Consequences, Encouragement, Maintenance I mentioned the strategy, "Catch "Em at the Door," I spoke of breaking the ice, in starting the class period on a positive note by sharing a positive interaction with each student as they're entering the classroom. A simple greeting, compliment, or word of encouragement sets the tone in building rapport in the teacher-student relationship. A simple but significant strategy shared in 2010 with colleagues when I was teaching at a different middle school where we were struggling with 90% of the staff being new to teaching or to the school community in establishing positive teacher-student rapport.

As I saw success with the strategy and shared it with my colleagues I discovered it had become a very popular means in changing both classroom and school environment climate. Is the educator solely responsible for creating an environment conducive for learning? During that same school year, I employed the strategy of putting the names of students on the board who were doing the right thing to motivate student cooperation. This is the same year I remember going home excited at the end of the day because I led instruction for a full 10 minutes! Influencing student cooperation and engagement was a tremendous challenge. As the students recognized my intention to consistently acknowledge and record names of students who demonstrated positive behavior more students began to take ownership of their behavior to receive the recognition. This also became a popular means by my colleagues that school year to help change classroom culture and school climate. Why is the promotion of student self-efficacy important for the educator in facilitating a culture conducive for learning within the classroom? I have also made it a consistent practice to express gratitude and appreciation to students and the entire classes when they display behaviors and actions that are aligned with procedures and expectations.

Are the students solely responsible for a classroom environment not being conducive for learning? "Technology is just a tool. In terms of getting the kids working together and motivating them, the teacher is the most important." – Bill Gates

A tactic vital to my success has been the deliberate articulation of the expected behaviors, and character traits required of my students. Words like focus, diligence, effort, and perseverance that I include in the warm-up, reinforce in the expectations of how they approach engaging with their work and in my conversations when critiquing their work. I have mentioned to others I don't teach art, I teach character and remind my students that, if they are willing to employ the proper strategies to do quality work I can teach them to do art. "The mediocre teachers tell. The good teacher explains. The superior teacher demonstrates. The great teacher inspires." – William Arthur Ward.

Be a teacher that inspires.

- *What components are essential in reinforcing the procedures and expectations of a culture conducive for learning?*

- *Would you consider using incentives to influence student engagement? Why, or why not?*

- *NEA.org 6 tips include:*
  1) take charge of your own class,
  2) focus on the disruptive students,
  3) let students choose their seats,
  4) give incentives to do their best on assignments,
  5) keep an eye on your students, and
  6) establish consequences for misbehavior.

- *Which do you currently do, and which are you willing to implement?*

DAY 20

Revived: Coping with Teacher Burnout

"The beautiful spring came; and when Nature resumes her loveliness, the human soul is apt to revive also."

Harriet Ann Jacobs

How do I recapture my joy and passion to teach when I feel drained and depleted? Two essential truths are gathered from reflecting upon Harriet Ann Jacobs' quote. There is a season in which the loveliness of the world around me fades like the colors of autumn into the dreariness of the monotone greys of winter. As new buds sprout and the precipitous winter weather transitions from snow and ice to sunshine, mixed with rain that nourishes the seedlings of hope and new life; my soul is refreshed with new vigor, perspective, and a resolve to finish strong as an educator. Recapturing the joy and passion of teaching is about cultivating one's heart and mind. It involves breaking up the hardened soil caused by cold winter storm winds of student apathy, student misconduct, lack of parental support, lack of administrative support, the hardened icicles caused by school district demands, and the overwhelming burdening feelings of inadequacy and a gnawing sense of hopelessness associated with the reality of being an educator. My colleague described it this way,

'I was shocked by how many students came from horrible circumstances beyond their control; from issues as wide ranging as having their electricity shut off to watching their mother beaten by a boyfriend. The more I came to realize just how many students are badly beaten down by their surroundings, the more I developed a sense of wonder at how resilient so many of my students were. As a teacher, once you lose a belief that there is a connection between what you do and the ultimate outcome, burnout

is sure to follow ... I believe burnout could have been delayed or averted if I had a better sense of life/work balance. When I didn't see meaningful results in student achievement, I doubled down on work, believing that an extra hour of planning, or a different approach would lead to the outcome I wanted for each of my students. Instead, what it did was accelerate my frustration, my sense of sinking.'

How do I draw the line at having compassion for what my students encounter when life happens and my limitations to help them that add to feeling overwhelmed? Consider these helpful tips that aid in enduring seasons of burnout:

> 1) Take inventory of thoughts/feelings through journaling to separate what is within your ability to resolve and where to let go.
>
> 2) Take and make time for self to be replenished, refueled, and reinvigorated.
>
> 3) Avoid the 'ongoing negative talk' associated with individual students, the school community, and the school system. Repetitive conversations about things out of your control exacerbates frustration and becomes cyclical and sickening to your own wellness. Anticipate as an educator the importance and necessity to refresh yourself to replenish your vitality to finish strong.

- *Why is it important to understand my limitations in what my students go through?*

- *Who, within the school and community, is accessible to address student concerns besides yourself to help alleviate feeling overwhelmed about your circumstances?*

- *Is it possible to integrate "principles of resiliency," or infuse them within classroom discussions as part of helping my students?*

DAY 21

Making Connection between Content and Clientele

"Kids need time for problem solving, critical thinking, applying knowledge through project-based instruction, working in teams, falling down and getting right back up to figure out what they didn't understand and why."

Randi Weingarten

What is the benefit of making connection between instruction and the student's prior knowledge, or life experience? Embedded in the answer to this inquiry is a challenge to the educator to have understanding of the content they teach, which allows for translation that consistently engages and challenges the student's initiative to learn. Transitioning from the reciting and recollection of facts to analyzing, synthesizing, and translating curriculum content into project-based instruction requires the educator to have his and her own understanding of how content is relative to real-world application. Mastering this skill empowers the classroom teacher to operate in the role of a facilitator - equipping, enabling, and empowering their students to make use of data and content (in a manner that they can then translate in creative, innovative ways) that reinforces and enhances their efficacy in the process of teaching and learning.

Understanding that my group of five eighth graders would be more resistant to hands-on, teacher directed instruction on creating a website, I allowed them to work at their own pace and create an outline of short term / long term goals required to create the marketing promotional tools for a student-led student training program they were implementing within their school community. It was a little unnerving watching them day to day, because you could see the actions and behaviors of procrastination associated with being unsure of where to begin, or reluctance in applying themselves to maximize the use of their time to engage in and participate in their own learning. By mid-quarter I showed them, according to their outline of goals what their current progress would look like if they were being graded and the leader of the group said they would have gotten a 'D' grade. From that point, they were more open to and willing to accept advice and helpful tips that aided them in completing all tasks in a timely manner and implementing a program that continues to operate though those five students are now in high school as ninth graders.

What do students gain from project-based instruction, or real-world application of content in curriculum instruction? Not all students do not have access to technology, even within the classroom, but all students have the capability to inquire, imagine, be innovative, and think creatively. The students who struggle to thinking creatively have become used to being told what the correct answer is, so they are not accustomed to instruction that offers more than one solution. Consider how math, reading language arts, science, social studies, and the arts content can be applied to some of the real-world challenges faced today. Strive to be an educator who facilitates the process of student efficacy and inspires learning.

- *What current real-world applications can you make in your curriculum instruction content?*

- *Have you ever invited your students to make suggestions on projects to apply to what they're learning or want to learn?*

- *How could students make use of their cell phones during classroom instruction?*

DAY 22

Empowerment- The Student's Role & Responsibility

"I tell a student that the most important class you can take is technique. A great chef is first a great technician. If you are a jeweler, or a surgeon or a cook, you have to know the trade in your hand. You have to learn the process. You learn it through endless repetition until it belongs to you."

Jacques Pepin

What is the better measure of a student's mastery of content:
  a) high score on an assessment, or
  b) the ability to translate content into real world application?

A teacher's efficacy in mastery of translating the content of the curriculum is essential to the student's efficacy in mastering the content. The more an educator excels in his or her ability to manage the dissemination of the content of the curriculum and effectively influences student cooperation in the procedures and expectations of the daily rituals and routines the more students become empowered to excel and thrive in their mastery of curriculum content. Helping students understand the necessity of the discipline associated with the process of teaching and learning influences a student's collaboration in embracing their role and responsibility in the process of teaching and learning. Whether the students are in math, art, science, or physical education, when they embrace the principles of focus, diligence, effort, and perseverance and how these principles are applied across varying content curriculum they position themselves for academic achievement and success. Some may think that all students would love a graphic-design class and readily cooperate because they have access to crayons and paint, and can doodle at will, but this is not always the case. I navigate and operate within my classroom to inspire my students to transcend their hesitancy to try or their fear of failure in drawing, using their imagination, and learning new concepts associated with the language of art by reinforcing the principles of focus, diligence, effort, and perseverance - daily. Instead of saying, 'stop talking," I will say, "Focus on your work." Daily warm up lessons will have embedded in them inquiries of how these principles become critical to the development of a quality artwork.

Why is it important to reinforce the expectations associated with teaching and learning every day? Helping a student embrace the effort and self-discipline in not talking while working independently to consistently achieve the best results in their work is as critical as producing the work. Their ability to access their imagination to be creative resides in their effort to engage with the process of the task. Tips for promoting student self-efficacy include:

1) Reinforcing belief in all student's ability to successfully complete tasks,

2) Embedding principles of character, like focus, in tasks associated with learning (define what being *on-task* looks like), and

3) Including rubrics that create clear and specific criteria to produce best results.

Create a classroom environment that promotes student self-efficacy, rewards, and consistently recognizes student initiative.

- *Do you believe all students have the ability to demonstrate appropriate classroom conduct consistently?*

- *Why is it helpful to talk beforehand, as well as have students write down, what the final product looks like?*

- *Why is it important to be consistent in explaining, reinforcing, and holding students accountable to classroom expectations?*

DAY 23

Perseverance

"Success is no accident. It is hard work, perseverance, learning, studying, sacrifice and most of all, love of what you are doing or learning to do."
Pele

What do you think contributes to long term success and fulfillment as an educator? Perseverance is the ability to continue steadily without giving up. The ability to endure is fueled by one's ability to persevere. At the heart of one's ability to persevere is their deliberate intent to demonstrate persistence. An educator's determination to make a difference has to exceed the reality of the challenges and oppositional forces associated with being a classroom teacher. No reality can be allowed to become greater than my ability to make a difference and impact my student's ability to engage, otherwise I will succumb to the feelings of resignation, cynicism, and defeat that threaten my joy, love for teaching, and passion to make a difference. Even in the face of the myriad of circumstances that can cause an educator to feel overwhelmed, momentarily defeated, or ineffective in making a difference, it is in those dark, difficult moments we summon the courage necessary to continue steadily, persevere, and endure until we regain momentum.

During my time as an educator, while writing the content for this book, I have discovered I have had multiple personal declarations that have aided me in my vision and mission of professional goals as a classroom teacher that fueled my drive and determination to experience fulfillment inside and outside the classroom.

My declarations since starting my career in 1992 included:
- a) 'Making a difference in the life of a child',
- b) 'Do as much as I could in the time I have outside the classroom to make a difference',
- c) 'Engage students in becoming positive contributors to their school community',
- d) 'Recapture the joy of being an educator',
- e) 'Teach my students to create quality, exemplary artwork that is used to communicate to the community',
- f) 'Promote and celebrate literacy', and
- g) 'Empower youth to be positive contributors to self, home, school, and community'.

Time and experience have taught me adaptability in identifying how I could make adjustments in my vision and mission of what I desired to accomplish with my students and helped me to pursue new ways of experiencing fulfillment that refueled my passion as an educator.

Is it loss of confidence to make a difference, or is it what's happening around me that threatens my passion to teach? At no time does an educator have any real power, or the ability to change the circumstances of their students, but within that classroom environment an educator is able to use their *'power'* to inspire, influence, and impact as many who are open to engage in the process of teaching and learning. Every day an educator stands in front of their students is another opportunity to make declarations consistently, creatively, and passionately to make a difference. Be deliberate and persistent in belief you will make a difference.

- *What do you notice begins to deplete you of passion and confidence to persist and persevere?*
- *How does consistent self-inventory aid you in rebuilding momentum when it's lost?*
- *What do you do to alleviate feeling overwhelmed, ineffective, or resigned to defeat?*

DAY 24

Rigor

"In my own life, when I was most inspired by a teacher, it always involved a real dialogue, a looseness and a real caring and compassion. It was not without rigor, not without discipline, not without standards, but all that was done out of love."

Michael Goldenberg

Do you have an understanding of 'rigor' that allows you to feel competent, comfortable, and confident in applying its meaning in the classroom, or explaining it to others? One of my 'professional frustrations' as an educator is the ongoing annual transition from previous terminology to new before the old is successfully adopted. Beyond this, another of my 'professional frustrations' lies in the inability to clearly articulate and explain this 'new' terminology in a way that makes it easily understandable, practical, and relatable to classroom teachers so they may effectively instruct their students. Rigor appears to be one of those concepts that sounds great in theory but appears to be awfully difficult to explain simplistically allowing for clarity and practical application.

At first glance, the word "rigor" does not appear to be a term one would easily associate with education, or classroom instruction, outside of "provision of greater, or more difficult work," and therein lies the problem. Without a simple, clearly defined meaning, rigor can be left up to one's interpretation and which breeds confusion and frustration. In order for my students to understand what I desired from them in expressing my desire for them to demonstrate effort towards their work, I discovered a definition that best describes how effort relates to art. One meaning of effort is the *power of the mind* and the *strength of the body* to complete a task. We would have a discussion of what the "power of the mind" includes to better understand how to equate it to effort and their work. Some of the thoughts included:

a) imagination,
b) memory,
c) thinking of ideas, and
d) visualizing.

I remind them it is difficult to effectively use the power of the mind without employing the *principle of focus* to consistently produce results that lead to quality, exemplary work. By reinforcing this definition of effort, I encourage my students to value the process of how an artist creates. Along with the skills involving art and graphic design, my students are learning the discipline of being creative.

Does the *meaning of rigor* sound similar to critical, or higher-order thinking? Even in art the application can be difficult for the student who is unaccustomed to using imagination or creative thinking. Couple this with a "fear of failure," or reluctance to apply effort because of an internal belief of being unable to draw, and art students show some of the same hesitancies as they would in math, science, or language arts. Journaling ideas, completing rough drafts, and using student examples to help inspire ideas helps students think creatively. Think creatively of how you can apply the meaning of rigor.

- *What are creative ways for students to demonstrate rigor within the discipline you teach?*

- *Does rigor require the students to explain how they come to the conclusion of what they're learning, or understanding?*

- *Can rigor include students using concepts of lesson to create real-life application of content, or real-world solutions to real world problems?*

DAY 25

Promoting Self-Efficacy

"People who have a sense of self-efficacy bounce back from failure; they approach things in terms of how to handle them rather than worrying about what can go wrong."

Albert Bandura

How can I proclaim my desired goals for my students that inspires and influences them to join me in the journey of mastering new skills? Each school year brings with it new challenges, new frontiers to explore, and new opportunities for growth, development, and maturity. In the process of this trek across the great expanse of transition and transformation from August to June, it would appear one common consistency from year to year is the need to engage youth in the process of teaching and learning. The educators who remains grounded in the understanding of their role and learns to master the various means by which this universal task is accomplished creates an ongoing momentum from year to year that fuels their passion and love for teaching. Classroom teachers who embraces the challenges associated with their role as an educator and can consistently face the daily grind of engaging youth in the process of teaching and learning are teachers who has mastered self-efficacy and can, thereby, instill the principles of self-efficacy within their students. At the heart of self-efficacy is the core belief in one's ability to do something and demonstrate independence in accomplishing the task.

The discipline and demonstration of self-efficacy requires the ability to model focus, effort, initiative, diligence, and perseverance. The educator who can verbalize daily, post visual reminders within the classroom environment, and provide meaningful feedback through handouts, the use of technology, and consistently offering incentives creates an environment that promotes self-efficacy. The history of our nation, in its secession from the influence of England, was a declaration of our independence, or a decree of our desire to demonstrate self-efficacy, or self-reliance apart from the influence of the rule of British control, or authority. A classroom operates most effectively and efficiently, without the constant oppositional disruption, when teachers can successfully invite students to join with them in collaborating to create an environment conducive to teaching and learning. This teaching style, over time, helps me to learn how to make my adversaries (students who misbehave) my allies, because they will learn to govern themselves consistently.

Does the teaching style that promotes self-efficacy mean no longer having to deal with oppositional, or disruptive behavior? The opportunity for disruption always exists. Promoting self-efficacy places the responsibility on the student to be accountable for his or her actions and the outcomes of those actions, including accepting consequences for misconduct. Time and experience reinforces to me the importance of planning for misbehavior, as I plan my daily lessons. Doing this consistently allows me to be prepared for the possibilities of misconduct that reinforces to the students the need to manage self. This consistency of response influences students to choose desired behaviors more often. Resolve to consider how you can promote self-efficacy within your classroom.

- *How do you currently promote self-efficacy in your classroom?*
- *Do you think teachers should be teaching character education principles, like focus, effort, etc., in the classroom?*
- *Are you consistent in explaining the desired behaviors required for your students to accomplish tasks and reinforce with consequences/incentives?*

DAY 26

Endurance

"To this end I labor, struggling with all his energy, which so powerfully works in me."
Colossians 1:29 NIV

What do you use as motivation to help you keep going, or regain momentum as the school year progresses? The famous saying, 'the ends justify the means,' comes to mind with regard to what one does to ensure fulfillment is accomplished in their personal success, achievement of goals, and aspirations to make progress with a given task. Words like struggle, sacrifice, determination, hard work ethic, diligence, effort, and perseverance come to mind on the subject of the lengths one would go to in seeking triumph, victory, and fulfillment in their quest to excel. I am reminded of the inspiration from scripture that proclaims, 'the race is not given to the swift, nor to the strong, but to the one who endures.' Achieving the end result of success and fulfillment at the end of each school year and over the course of their career requires the utmost commitment of the educator to his or her craft. The means by which this course is endured and completed requires a strong mental stamina and internal resolve that outlasts the obstacle course of challenges and opposition that threaten to thwart a classroom teacher's motivation to stay the course and win the race.

To fight the good fight and keep the faith requires determination, drive, an initiative mindset, a vision, and mission that fuels the educator's motivation to keep going when the going gets tough. Our 'true grit' as an educator is forged in outlasting the myriad of challenges and oppositional forces that threaten to steal our joy and passion to teach and through it all we remain steadfast, strong, immovable, and unshaken. Six years since returning to the classroom, after being out of the classroom for 10 years of my career, I no longer desire to leave the classroom. It was an arduous struggle making the mental, emotional adjustment to the transition occurring in my life returning to the classroom in 2010, but I have never felt more at rest and fulfilled, since returning, than I do right now. It was important to me in 2010 to recapture the joy and love for being in the classroom, but the resignation and disillusionment felt in having to return was intense. It was important for me in 2010 to get to the 'better place.'

Do you feel like you've "lost that lovin' feeling" towards being an educator? In 2010-2011 and since being at my current school community, one thing that has aided my motivation to recapture my joy and love for being in the classroom was identifying professional colleagues who excelled at being classroom teachers that fueled me to want to do the same. This reminds me of the biblical principle, "As iron sharpens iron, so one man sharpens another" (Proverbs 27:17). Desiring to feel better, be better, and achieve more helped too. Ongoing self-inventory will empower you to thrive and be your optimal best.

- *What qualities do you see in your professional colleagues you could benefit from employing, or improving?*

- *In how you work with your students, where do you see room for improvement?*

- *What part of the duties (lesson planning, classroom management, etc.) of being an educator can you benefit from fine tuning?*

DAY 27

Interdisciplinary Approach

"Kids need time for problem solving, critical thinking, applying knowledge through project-based instruction, working in teams, falling down and getting right back up to figure out what they didn't understand and why."

Randi Weingarten

Would the interdisciplinary approach to instruction include of the concept of rigor? The teachers I admire as a professional colleague are those educators who seem to have mastered their ability to make instruction relevant, relatable, and successfully reinforce the desired expectations of student behavior in a way that creates a classroom environment where students display enjoyment in being there. When I talk with my students about subjects they enjoy, the consistent reply to "why?" is in acknowledgement that the teacher makes the learning fun, or the "process of teaching and learning" is enjoyed. There is an understood balance between the role of the educator in how content is presented and the student's role in engaging in the lesson, along with the student's clear understanding misbehavior is not acceptable and will incur consequences.

Within the word "interdisciplinary" is the word "discipline," which is understood to mean "to teach," so instruction is enhanced, or becomes more meaningful, relatable, or relevant when it can be connected to other disciplines outside of the core content area or associated with real life application. Innovation within the classroom involves instruction that inspires inquiry, problem solving, and real-world application engaging student initiative in the process of problem solving. Inside and outside of the classroom, the past 4 years,

I have sought to achieve this as the graphic design teacher by:

1) using of iMovie program on computers for students to create video commercials, or documentaries on topics of interest to them (i.e., bullying, friendship, hip hop music, etc.),
2) partnering with the local library and community center to have student artwork displayed within the community,
3) collaborating with the guitar teacher so art/guitar students could create abstract art inspired from instrumental music,
4) inviting students to create posters to display within the school community promoting mental health awareness annually during the month of May, and
5) inviting staff, students, and community to participate in the promotion and celebration of literacy through creative writing contests, an evening public speaking event, and student volunteerism involvement in local interschool community activities.

Is it necessary to include the student's interests in the presentation of instruction? At the beginning of every semester I invite my students to make a list of 26 things they like ranging from favorite food to favorite music to favorite color and so on. As we begin to identify inspiration, ideas, and thoughts about the various projects we will work on, I refer them back to the list to identify how they can make use of their interests within their artwork. Having this list decreases the number of students plagued by the "brain freeze dilemma" of not knowing what to do. Determine how to promote the interdisciplinary approach to your classroom instruction daily.

- *How could you make connection between your content area and another content to make instruction relatable and relevant?*

- *Where can the student's interests be integrated within the lesson planning of your content area?*

- *Can you involve another professional colleague in a project-based lesson related to your content, or invite someone from the community who can help students see the connection, or relevance to your content area?*

DAY 28

Making Allies out of Adversaries

"The whole point of Superman, as originally created, was to be the ally of those who had no other allies. It put that magnitude of power, the most powerful guy in the world, in the service of those who had no hope, no chance."

J. Michael Straczynski

When misconduct arises in the classroom, is it the student, or the misbehavior that becomes the adversary? Though we are not "Superman or Wonder Woman" as educators, part of our role and responsibility as a classroom teacher is to rally our students as allies united in the goal of excelling in the daily tasks of teaching and learning. Understanding this, the educator needs to consider, on the subject of allies and adversaries, whether the goal is to win every battle - or to win the war.

Whether I see the adversary as the student, or the misconduct, my goal as the classroom teacher is to gain the student's cooperation and willingness to participate and engage consistently in the process of teaching and learning. This requires strategy on the part of the classroom teacher to communicate and interact with students consistently in a way that inspires, influences, and motivates students to relinquish desires and motivation to disrupt and adopt behaviors that make them consistently positive contributors to themselves and the classroom community. I can't mistreat, belittle, demean, disrespect, or disregard a student by means of punishment for misconduct and expect them to want to willingly cooperate with me. Means by force, or control, to subdue a student by one's authority creates an environment full of discord, tension, and incites rebellion. Hardly an environment conducive for learning. I learned to think of discipline as what I desired to do with the child to help them cooperate instead of what I desired to do to them because of how I felt. I am one who used to break yardsticks and use angry yelling as a means for correction and discipline, but wisdom, time, and experience have taught me that this does not work long term. It's unprofessional, and unhealthy for everyone exposed to the behavior. Maintaining control of my thoughts, emotions, perceptions, and patience empowers me now to ride out the momentary storm of disruption, while determining my course of action of discipline, that will enable students and me to arrive at the desired goal together of winning the war *"to cooperate and participate."*

Which battles must be won, compromised, and surrendered in order to win the war of inspiring students to become allies instead of adversaries? Understanding that I can't control my students, I have taken the first step of acceptance of my limitations. This puts the responsibility of managing behavior where it belongs: with the student. Clear, specific consistent expectations reinforce students' need to cooperate and participate. Preparedness and follow through with consistent consequences for misconduct consistently helps the student who tests boundaries. Resolve to make allies out of your classroom adversaries.

- *Is there a difference between what I do "with a child," or do "to a child" regarding consequences, or discipline because of misconduct?*

- *What is the value of learning to communicate clear, specific expectations and procedures daily involving instruction?*

- *When you become angry and desire to yell, how can you avoid making this a habit of professional practice?*

DAY 29

Manifestation Mindset

"It is written: "I believed; therefore, I have spoken." Since we have that same spirit of faith, we also believe and therefore speak."

2 Corinthians 4:13 NIV

Have you ever thought about what you desired your students to take away from being taught by you? Whether it is a conscious reflection, or subconscious act motivated internally from one's deliberation to excel, having a vision and mission filled purpose as an educator can be inspiring, influential, and impactful. So much of what an educator does within the classroom setting goes far beyond the content of the subject they teach. The opportunity to educate and the power of affecting and influencing the minds of youth brings with it a huge challenge and responsibility. Understanding this, the educator who excels is the teacher who embraces the challenge, accepts the responsibility, and engages their students in the outcomes of the daily tasks associated with teaching and learning.

I am reminded of the power of the tongue principle in reflection on the topic of declaration and in reflection I thought about what entails using my words, or the power of the tongue, to inspire, influence, and impact. Personal accountability to the power of the tongue requires me to be accountable to:

    1) the power of my thoughts and emotions,

    2) perceptions,

    3) beliefs,

    4) presence, and

    5) actions, that all influence my words and my students.

One example recently I have seen this play out in my classroom over the past 4 years was in announcing to my students the desire and ambition to make a movie having access to iMovie technology on the Mac computers we have access to as the graphic design teacher. Over the past 4 years, two sets of students have positioned themselves with support from their peers to actively involve themselves in bringing this idea into fruition. A sixth-grade student wrote her script during the summer of 2016, organized an enthusiastic group of friends, as seventh-grade, of the same mindset to commit time after school to film it during this past school year 2016-2017, and are on pace to complete production by the end of her eighth-grade year 2017-2018. She was the lead actress in the first student's movie project. They fell short of completing production of the filming, but continues the legacy left by previous student.

Am I impairing or empowering my students by the power of my tongue? What I believe about my role, my students, and my ability to affect change ultimately plays out in how I teach and lead my students in instruction. As one who had to learn to recapture the joy of teaching I understand how the symptoms of burnout can affect performance and passion. Consistently, over the past 25 years, I have seen the value of self-inventory and personal accountability in helping me remain confident in what I do while adjusting to change. Be accountable to what is required to excel in your role as an educator.

- *What is important to me that my students take away from being taught by me?*
- *What ways can I communicate my aspirations and ambition as an educator to my students?*
- *What does making a declaration mean to you as an educator?*

DAY 30

Differentiating: Teaching to Their Intelligence

"At the age of six I wanted to be a cook. At seven I wanted to be Napoleon. And my ambition has been growing steadily ever since."
Salvador Dali

Are you familiar with the multiple intelligence theory developed by Howard University professor of education Dr. Howard Gardner in 1983? Dr. Gardner cites 8 distinct intelligences associated with children and learning:
    1) linguistic (words),
    2) logical (math),
    3) spatial (images),
    4) kinesthetic (body),
    5) music,
    6) interpersonal (relating to others),
    7) intrapersonal (relating to self), and
    8) naturalist (relating to nature).

Combining the concepts of rigor and the interdisciplinary approach to classroom instruction reinforces the theory of these eight components of intelligence. Considering how to incorporate these components into instruction can lead to a higher degree of student engagement and innovation resulting in greater long-term, of exemplary learning outcomes. The multiple intelligence theory also reinforces the reality of each student being different in how they learn and engage in the world around them that makes them feel empowered, capable, and connected. Respecting the reality of different learning styles, at every level, influences the educator to look at relevant means by which instruction is delivered that inspires learning. This speaks to the heart of what encompasses being a classroom teacher.

Knowledge of content is unimportant to the student if the information cannot be disseminated consistently in a manner that makes it tangible, enjoyable, and memorable. Much like the professional head coach who is able to adjust his or her style of coaching in a manner that fits the personality and ability of the players that empowers them to succeed, the classroom teacher must facilitate content in whatever manner that elevates their students to new heights of innovation and problem solving. Inside the classroom I have seen this impact in the students using the iMovie program to make video commercials, documentaries, and public-service announcements (PSAs). Outside the classroom this impact has been accomplished by engaging the students in discussions leading to real-world application of creating opportunities for student service that promotes volunteerism for their peers within the school and community. Both of these activities engage the students in critical thinking, strategic planning, and problem solving during the process of producing their final product or rendering their act of service.

Does every lesson have to incorporate all 8 components associated with the multiple intelligence theory? The use of the iMovie program allows students to use images, words, video content, music (audio), and their unique sense of imagination and creativity to communicate topics of interest to them. This is allowing students to learn how to use technology, influenced from what they watch every day at home, to be creative in translating what they learn in the classroom. The difference now is that they are the ones producing the content instead of always looking at someone else's. Finding constructive ways of including their fascination with technology can enhance their engagement in learning the content. Students benefit from peer tutoring, so creating a means for students to help one another, which can also inspire growth in student achievement. Assisting their peers reinforces their understanding of daily instruction. Challenge yourself to identify innovative ways to promote multiple intelligence instruction.

Cortland Jones

- *Do you see a connection between rigor, an interdisciplinary approach, differentiated instruction, and the multiple intelligence theory?*

- *Which of the 8 intelligences do you use most in your method of instruction and which would you consider adding moving forward?*

- *What is one project-based assignment related to your content that you could implement that uses multiple intelligence components?*

DAY 31

Community Requires Unity

"Unity is strength... when there is teamwork and collaboration, wonderful things can be achieved."
Mattie Stepanek

What components are essential to an educator to inspire unity between themselves and their students? At the core of the principle of unity is agreement. Misconception suggests that unity means sameness. Unity brings the collective core of differences towards the focal point of a collective goal. Understanding each component's responsibility to ensure progress and success in the fulfillment of the group's united vision and mission is essential to achieving unity. Each individual, albeit different in composition, exemplifies agreement in the demonstration of identified core concepts required to accomplish the goals and objective while maintaining individual personality characteristics. Each in turn assumes a measure of accountability, responsibility, and role of leadership that requires each individual to cooperate and participate in the principle of unity, while working together towards progress and success.

The challenge of the educator is resisting the impulse to demand sameness in pursuit of the goal over agreement. Understanding leadership is exemplified in various ways. Each individual student, along with the teacher, is a classroom leader in accomplishing the demonstration of unity. The goal is influencing each leader to be in agreement to work together in accomplishing the daily goals and objectives of teaching and learning within the classroom environment. The child who talks a lot will always talk a lot and the child who is quiet will always be quiet, but each student needs to agree to what unity requires to achieve regarding cooperation and participation during instruction time. Not all students want to help in cleaning up, but each shares this responsibility to. All students want to run errands, but all are not responsible with the privilege. The educator's ability to consistently articulate, model, and reinforce the principles of unity, agreement, cooperation, and participation determines his or her success in inspiring and influencing their student's willingness to demonstrate unity. For a period of 30-40 minutes daily, I challenge my students to demonstrate focus, effort, diligence, and perseverance towards their work. My talkers are not always willing to agree with this request evidenced by their inability to stop talking. I may offer incentives, employ the reinforcement of desired behavior by announcing consequences, or invite the talkers to a challenge of working independently for 5-10 minutes to aid them in demonstrating the principle of agreement. Each day has its own outcome.

Have you ever discussed, before independent practice begins, what behaviors the students would need to model, or why they're important to the lesson? The understanding of a concept is demonstrated by actions that demonstrate the value of what is understood. Consistently embedding within my daily dialogue the "why?" behind the need for agreement, cooperation, and participation engages more students to comply. Recognition and reward of the demonstrated behaviors that exemplify agreement reinforces the motivation to repeat the desired behaviors. This builds momentum in students demonstrating unity. So now, students look to pursue cooperation and participation as individual goals during the process of teaching and learning. This is at the heart of character education. Be intent to articulate, model, and reinforce principles of unity.

Of the three:
    1) articulate,
    2) model, and
    3) reinforce,

    which could you become more consistent in promoting the principle of unity?

- *Do you think it's necessary to recognize and reward students for cooperating and participating during instruction time?*

- *What are ways to recognize and reward without having to invest a lot of money towards treats?*

Dedication

Giving honor to God and my Lord and Savior Jesus Christ without Whom there is no source or resource of grace and inspiration for me to write and share with others what He has graciously given me. Since the Spring of 1993, when I came to know God through faith in Jesus Christ, my journey in being an educator, since October 1992, has paralleled my growth and development in learning to walk by faith. A sojourn enjoyed immensely, both as an educator and Christian, that unfolded before me great moments of highs and lows like a great storybook, or dramatic performance.

The year I was recognized by one of my former students as 1 of 2 most influential teachers in her life affirmed my fulfillment in wanting to make a difference in the life of a child when I started my career. Another of my students sought me out as a young adult to share how my conduct, as a Christian educator, inspired her as a middle school student and professing Christian. I marveled at hearing this considering I had just committed my life to Christ at the time I instructed this student in my classroom. Twenty-three years into my journey, in the Spring of 2015, I was awarded with an ACE Educators Award in Greenbelt, Maryland that I received as affirmation from God of my effort to honor my role as an educator in service and support to the school and community of Greenbelt, as well as the time invested in commitment to the role and responsibility of being a classroom teacher.

Within the past year of writing this book I learned it was my mother's dream to be a classroom teacher. In honor of her life sacrificed to ensure she could provide for her four children that didn't afford her the opportunity to pursue her dreams, I dedicate this book to my mother. A woman of great humility, compassion, and kindness, who did serve two years in a daycare facility teaching pre-kindergarteners, who embodies the spirit of an educator in how she lives and gives of herself to others in the school of life. She continues to teach me lessons of patience, generosity, gentleness, meekness, strength, and love. Through the spirit of what she desired to be I have been blessed to follow the way of the educator and benefit from her life lessons passed on to my own two children and the countless children I teach. My mother's life is a sermon to me about maintaining an attitude of contentment in the face of difficulty and challenging circumstances as a two time breast cancer survivor, one who has known victory over diabetes, and has endured the adversity of separation, divorce, homelessness, and mental illness. Through it all she responds to life with an open heart and open mind allowing the inspiration of faith and grace to keep her going. Be inspired by the Apples of Grace shared as you read this book.

Thank You Notes

To the following I express my sincere appreciation and gratitude for your support of me and affirmation that has fueled me in my journey as an educator, writer, and follower of Christ:

Thank you, Shannon Baylor-Henderson, as my coach and editor helping me to identify my writing style, develop my craft, and complete this project. Your success as a professional writer gave me the ability to see what I aspire to accomplish is achievable and your support gave me goals and steps to help me get there.

Thank you, Altamese Thompkins Larkins, for your light, energy, and enthusiasm that fueled me during the journey of completing this project and for agreeing to write the foreword. We just met, but it feels like we have been friends forever.

Thank you, Markell West for your professional support during first stage of editing that fueled my efforts to keep the momentum of the project moving forward.

Thank you, Dion and Christine of Jay Media Publishing for coming alongside me to support my journey as an author to help continue my aspirations as a published author.

Thank you, Shauna F. King, as my friend and colleague in the field of education for over 20 years you have been a source of affirmation and motivation whose life, truly, has influenced many of the pathways that contributed to who I am today as a professional, educator, and entrepreneur.

Thank you, Kathleen Arban, for the many conversations that were instrumental in aiding me find my 'better place' and fulfillment as a writer. Your listening ear enabled me to begin and complete the journey of my first published book and your friendship has been an invaluable blessing.

Thank you, Ashley N. Lam, for honoring me as 1 of 2 educators who influenced your life. Educators are not always aware of the impact they make, but your recognition affirmed my ambition to make a difference in the life of a child. Thank you for allowing me to be a part of your life.

Thank you, Sommer Sasscer-Clark, for your initiative to seek me out, as an adult, to tell me how my conduct as an educator inspired you as a professing Christian when you were in middle school. Your presence in my life is a testament to who I strive to be as a child of God and a gentle reminder of how far I've come, as a classroom teacher, after leaving you in DC on my first field trip. LOL

Thank you, Anna L. and Julie D., for being educators who motivated me to reclaim my 'why?' when returning to the classroom was a difficult transition.

Thank you, Charles Bey, for being sincere to dialogue with me about the content of my books that aided me in my journey.

Thank you, Melissa E. and the Greenbelt Community Foundation, for your support of the vision and mission of the GMS Art, Literature, Leadership initiative providing over $9,000.00 in grant funding to aid me and my nonprofit The Better Place, Inc. in supporting the community of Greenbelt.

Thank you, Rosalind Caesar and the Advisory Committee on Education (ACE) of Greenbelt, for honoring me with the ACE Educators Award in the Spring of 2015 that validated my years of service to Prince George's County Public Schools.

Thank you, Paul Lewis, my first principal who hired me as an art teacher at James Madison Middle School in the Fall of 1992 and nominated me for a First Year Teacher's Award.

Thank you, to my family, friends, and colleagues who have cheered me on and come alongside me as I have sojourned in seeking to be a light to make the world around me a better place.

www.ingramcontent.com/pod-product-compliance
Lightning Source LLC
Chambersburg PA
CBHW020702300426
44112CB00007B/482